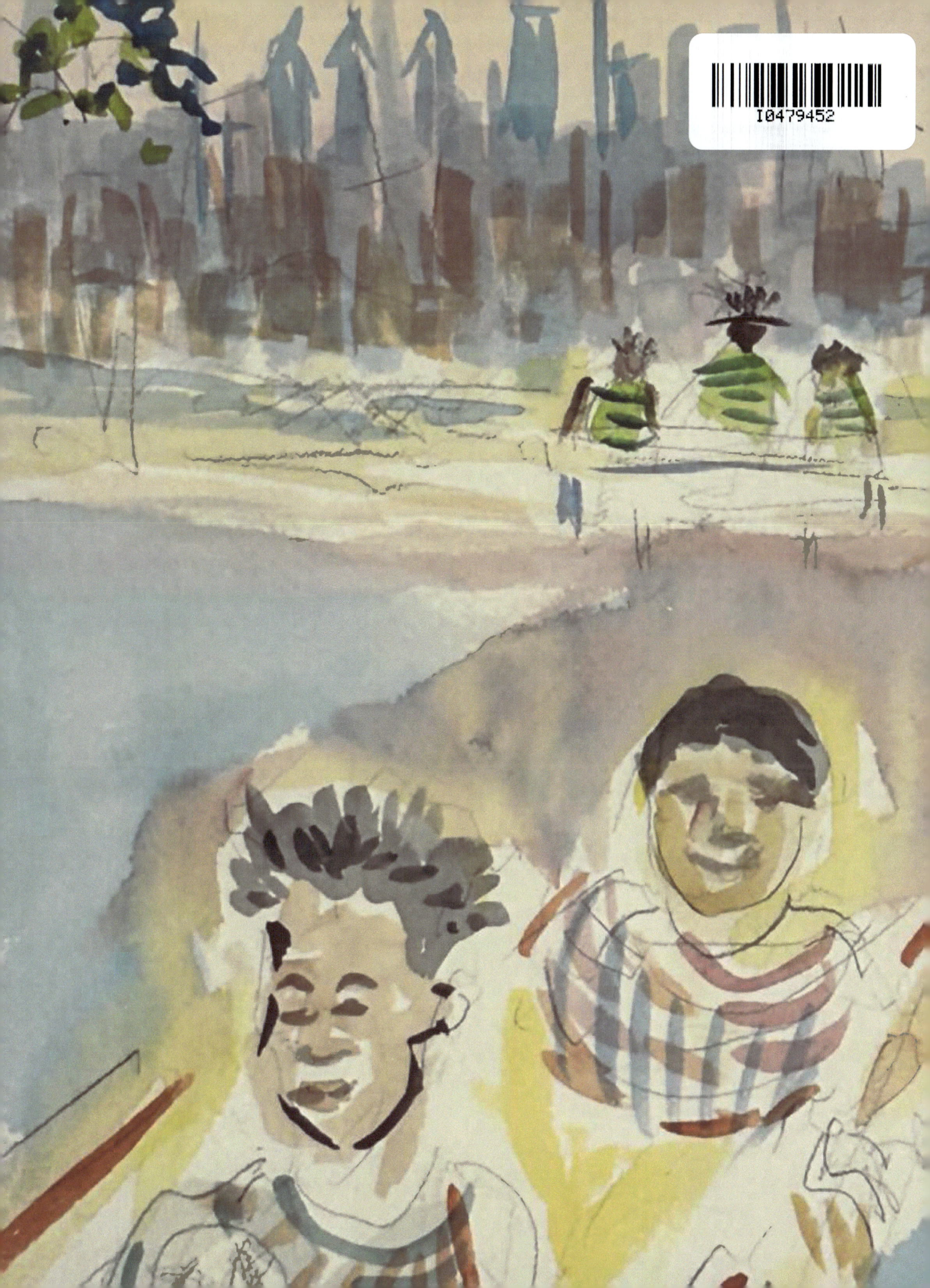

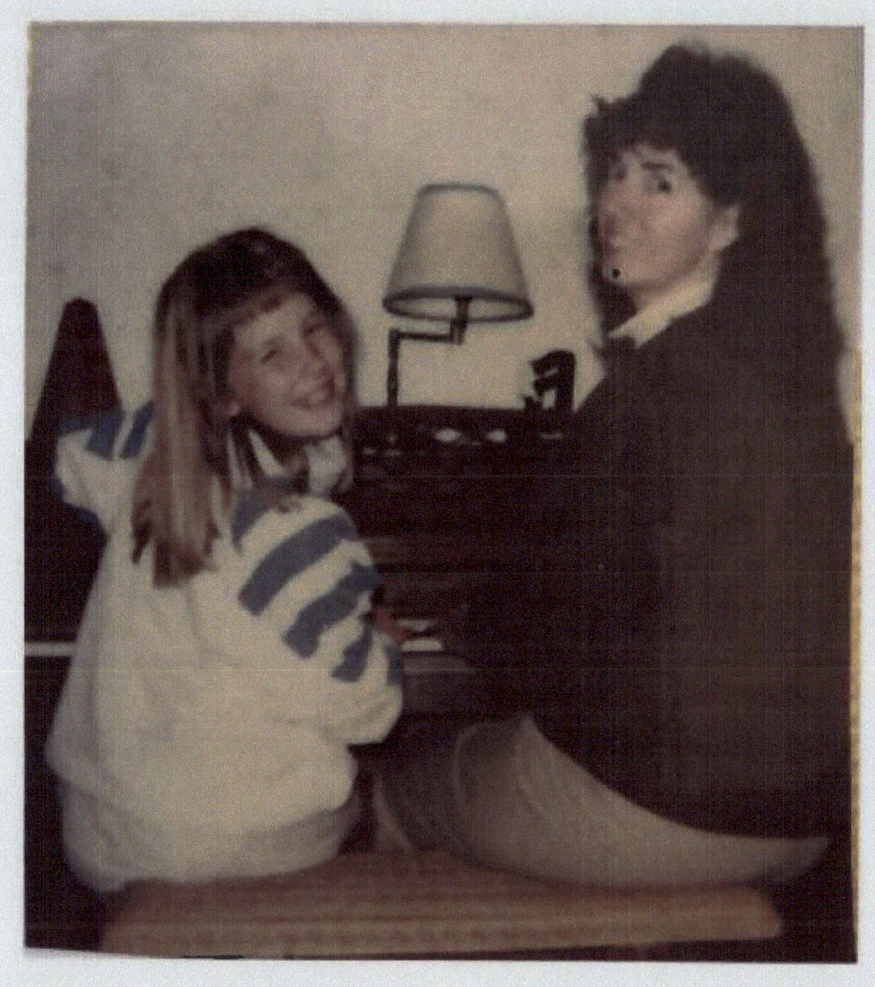

This book is dedicated to my
Aunt Sandy - thank you for
sharing your light and
laughter with me. You are
beautiful inside and out!

Mr. Joe Mr. Joe
what are you doing
today?

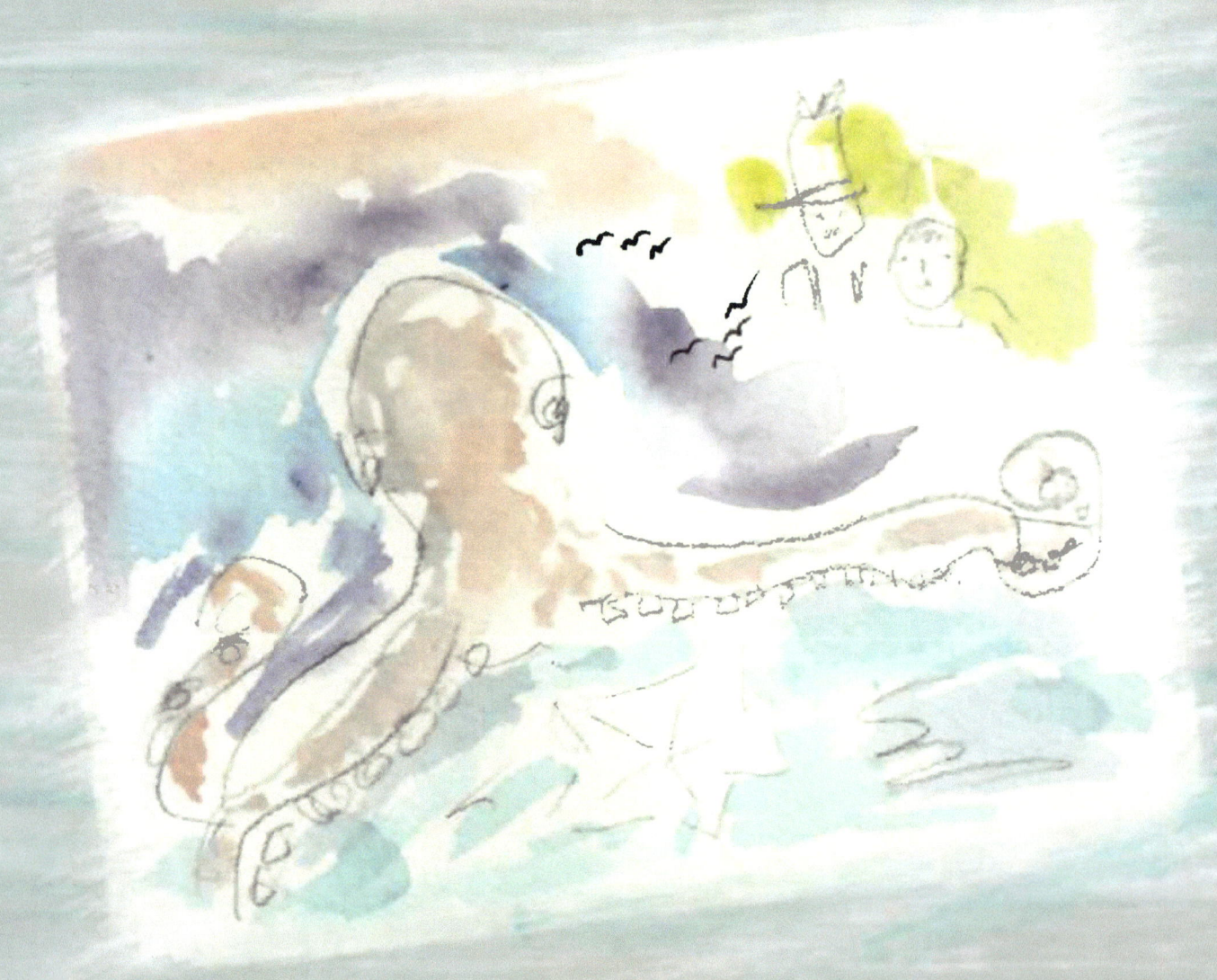

We want to go to the aquarium - what do you say?

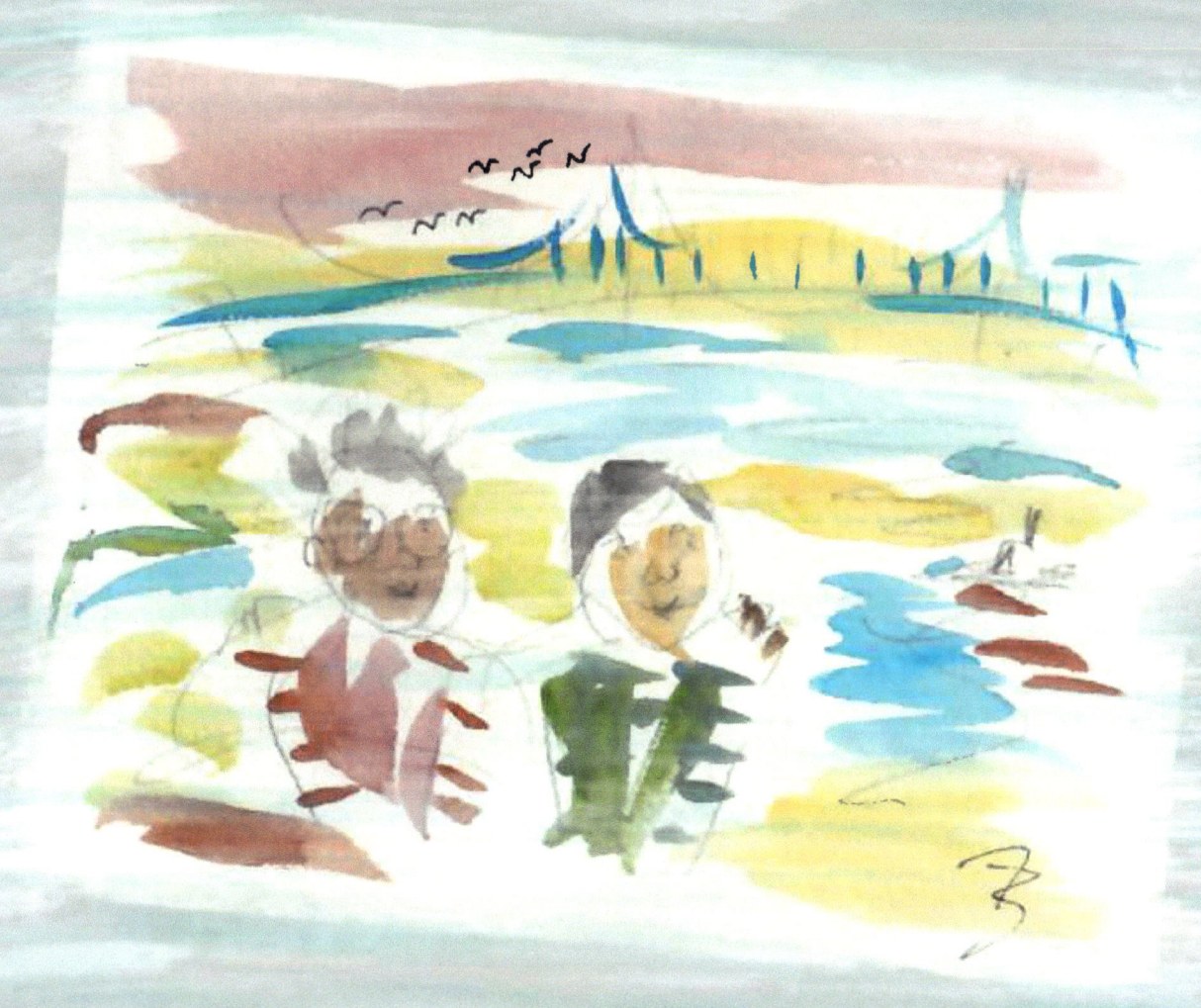

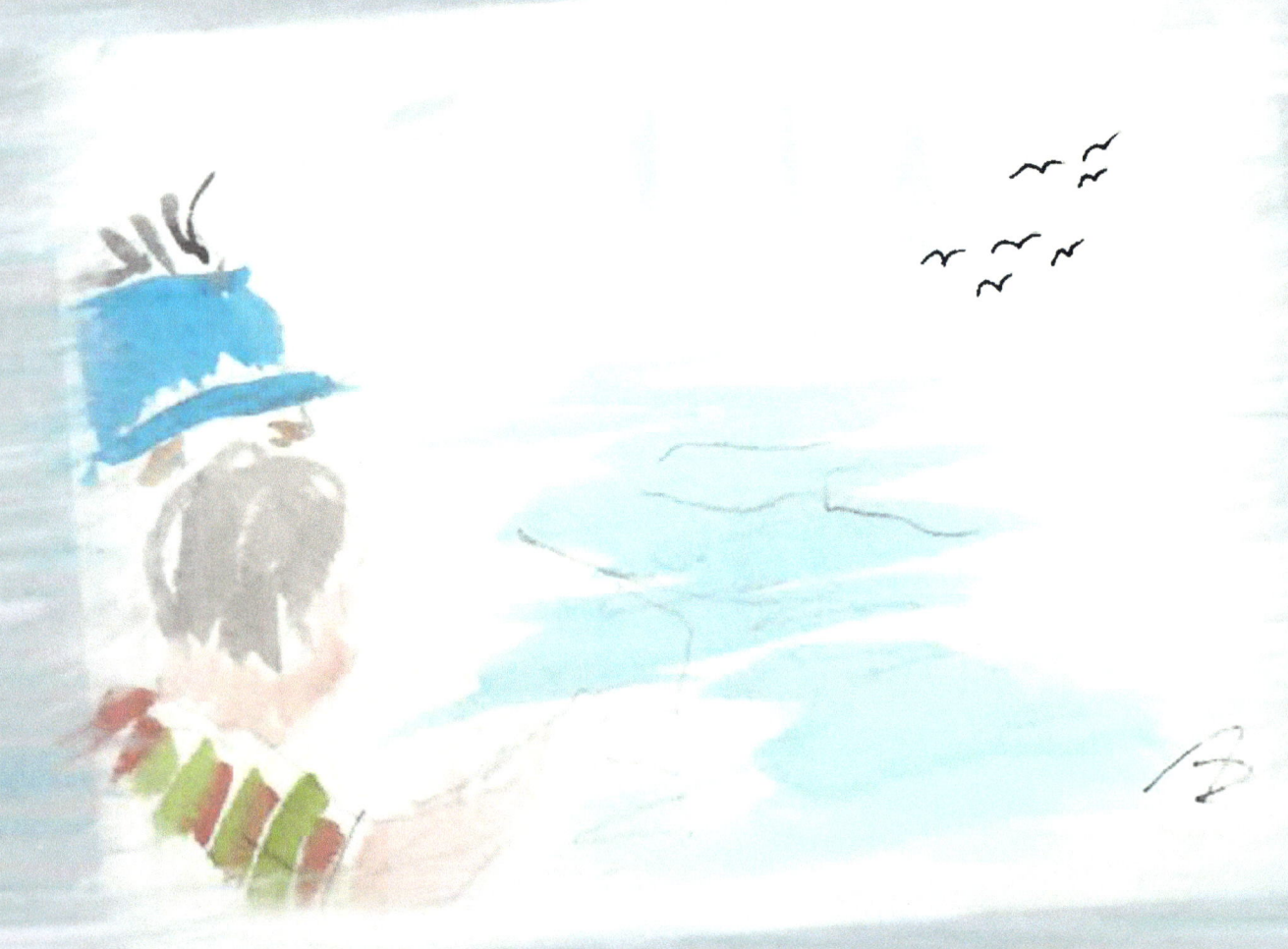

Mr. Joe Mr. Joe
first we can go and check
out the sting ray pool.

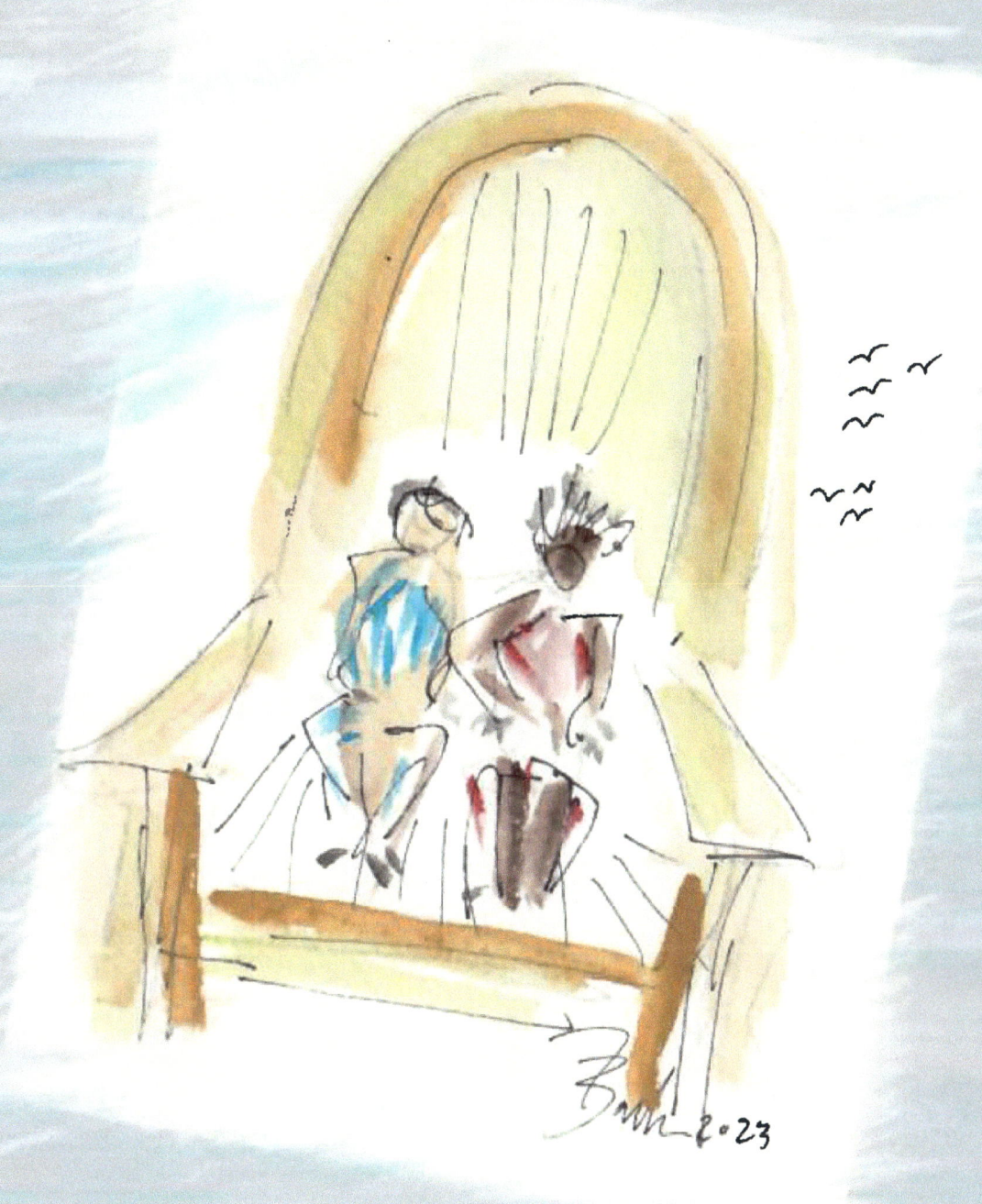

Don't be a scardy cat go
ahead and touch them -
they feel pretty cool!

Mr. Joe Mr. Joe
can we go outside where it
is hot and smells far from
delish?

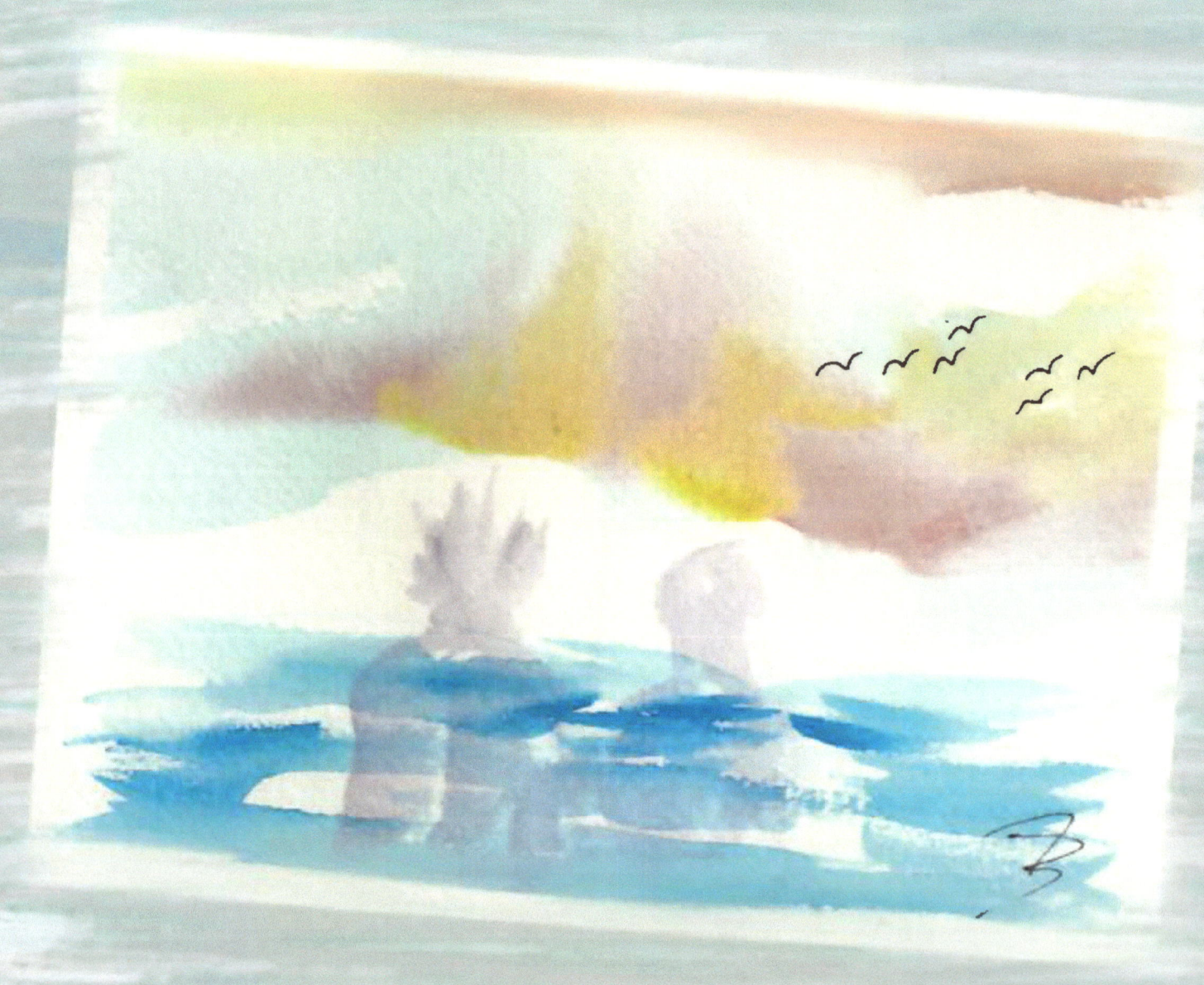

Don't be silly, it isn't dirty - it's penguins being fed fish!

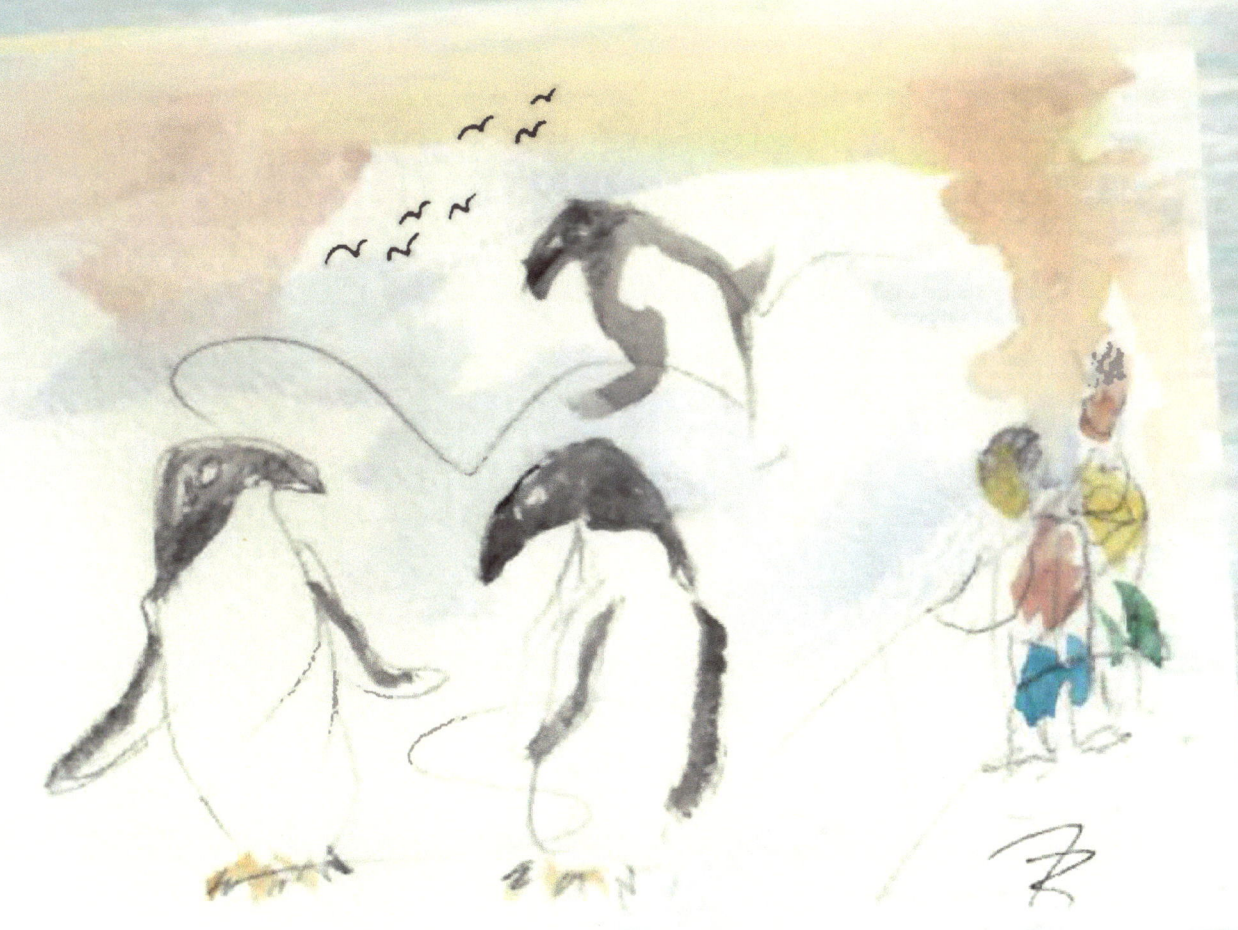

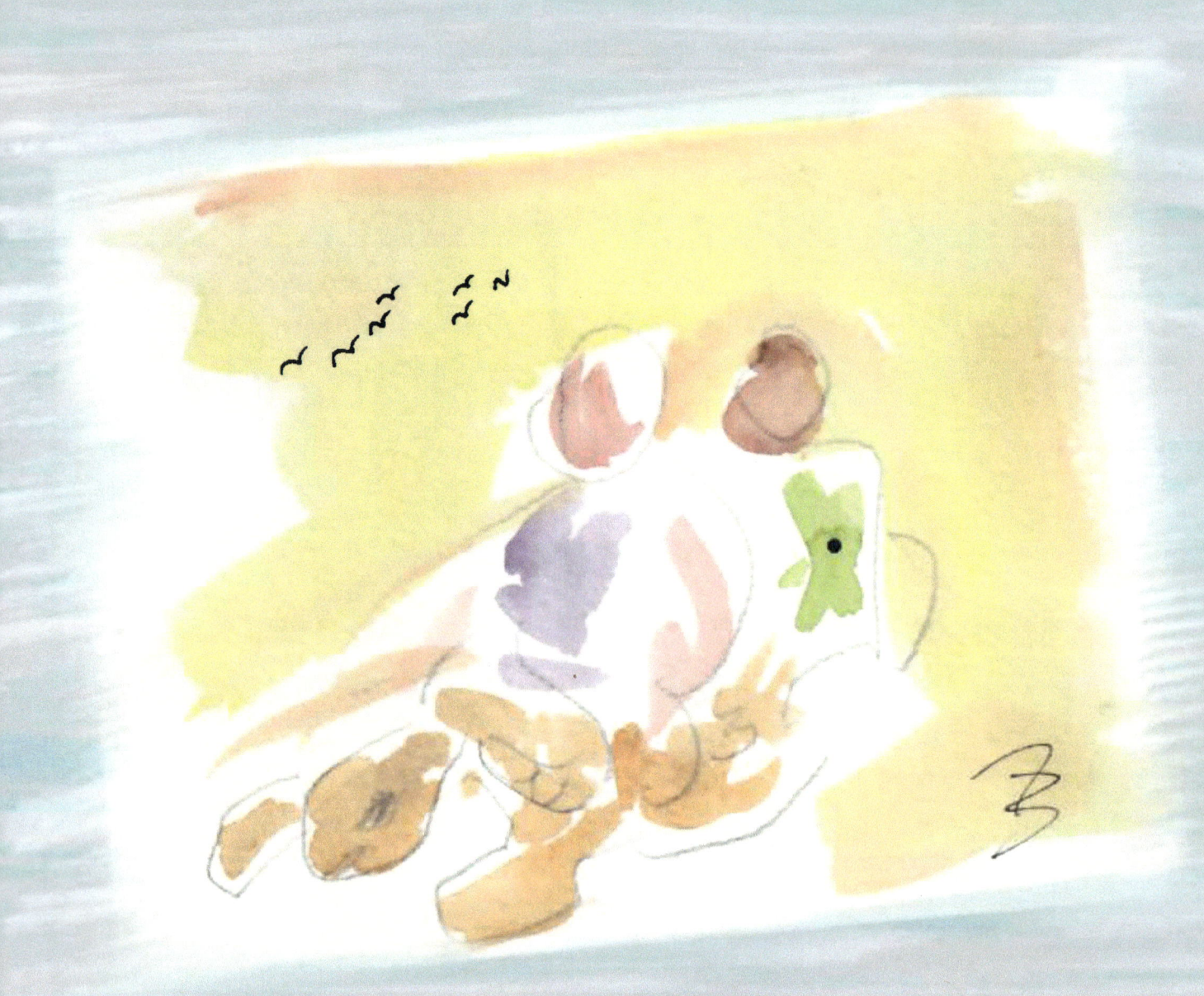

Mr. Joe Mr. Joe
after that let's race to the
elevator and go up a floor.

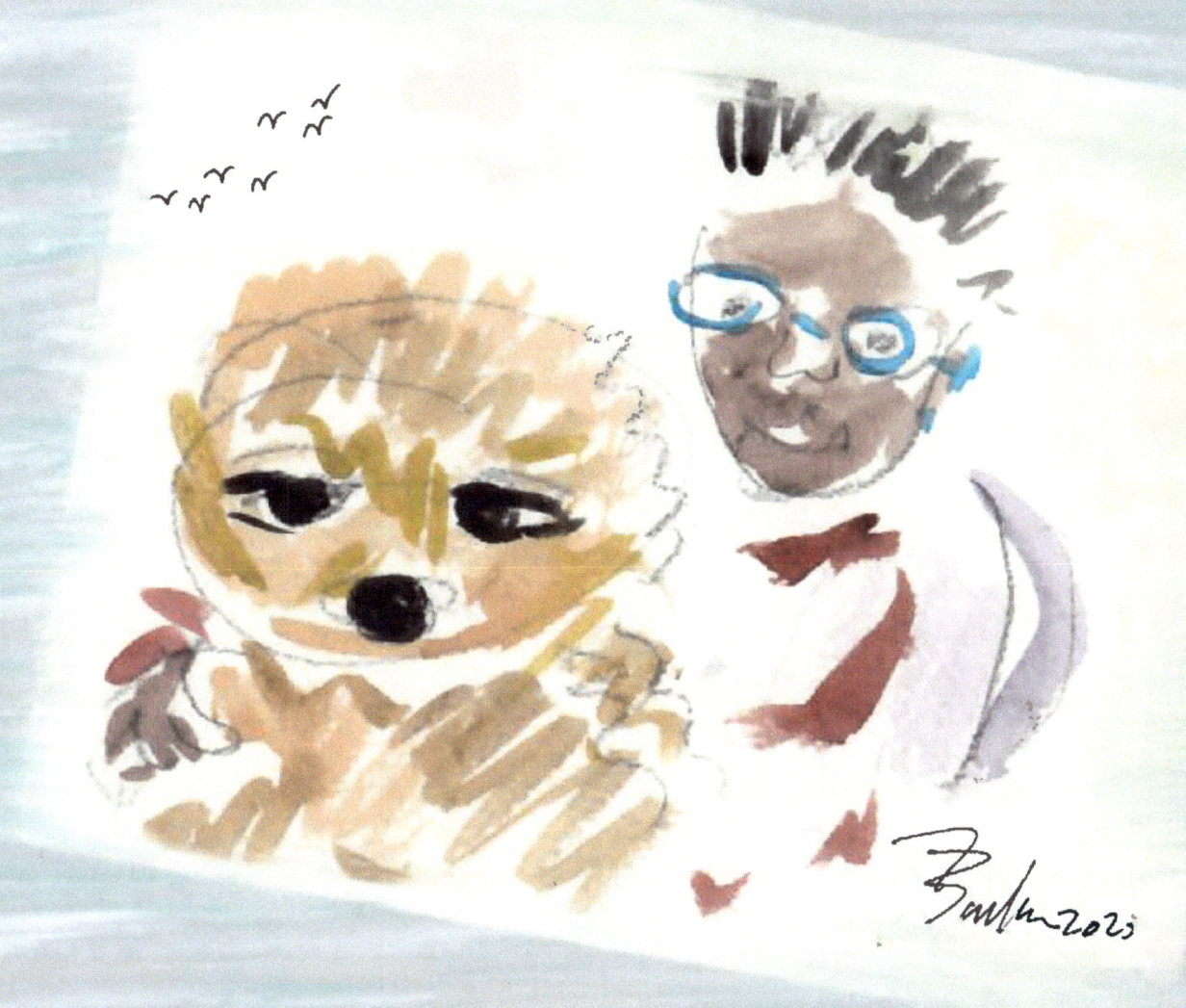

Up there we can pet a
starfish, look at frogs and
so much more!

Mr. Joe Mr. Joe
you climbed aboard our
boat for an adventurous
ride.

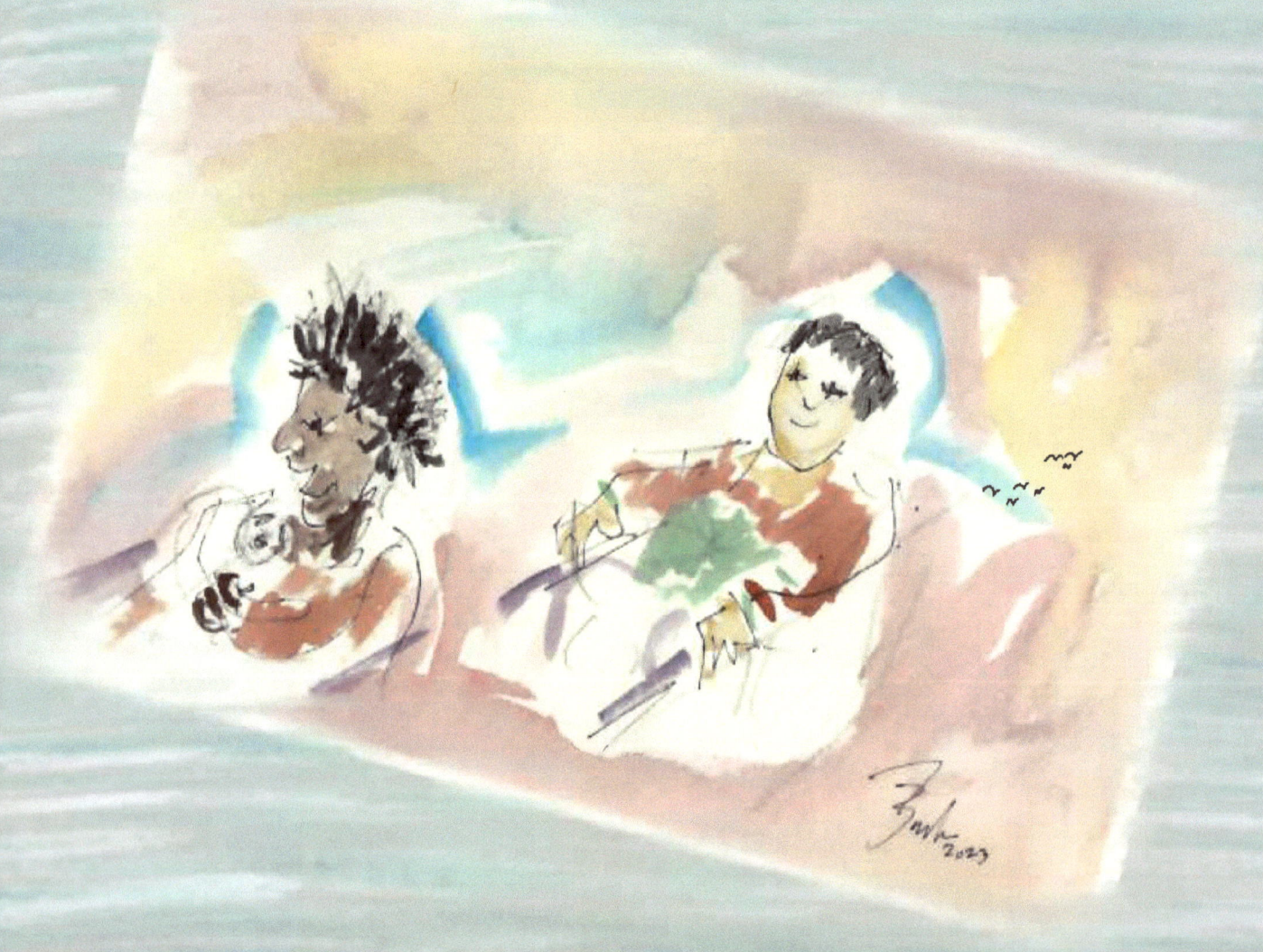

The way we were steering, if it was on the water, you would've fallen off the side!

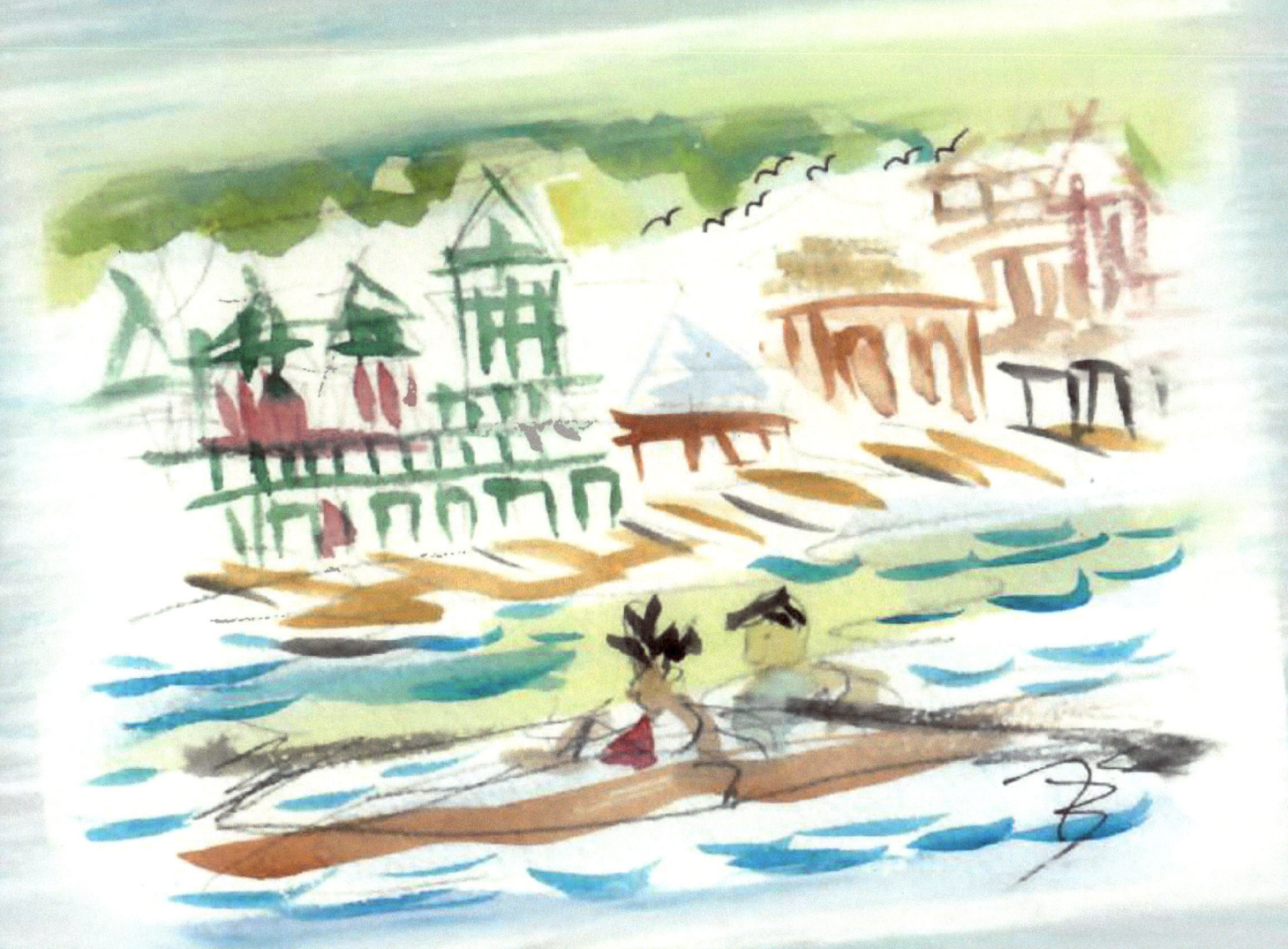

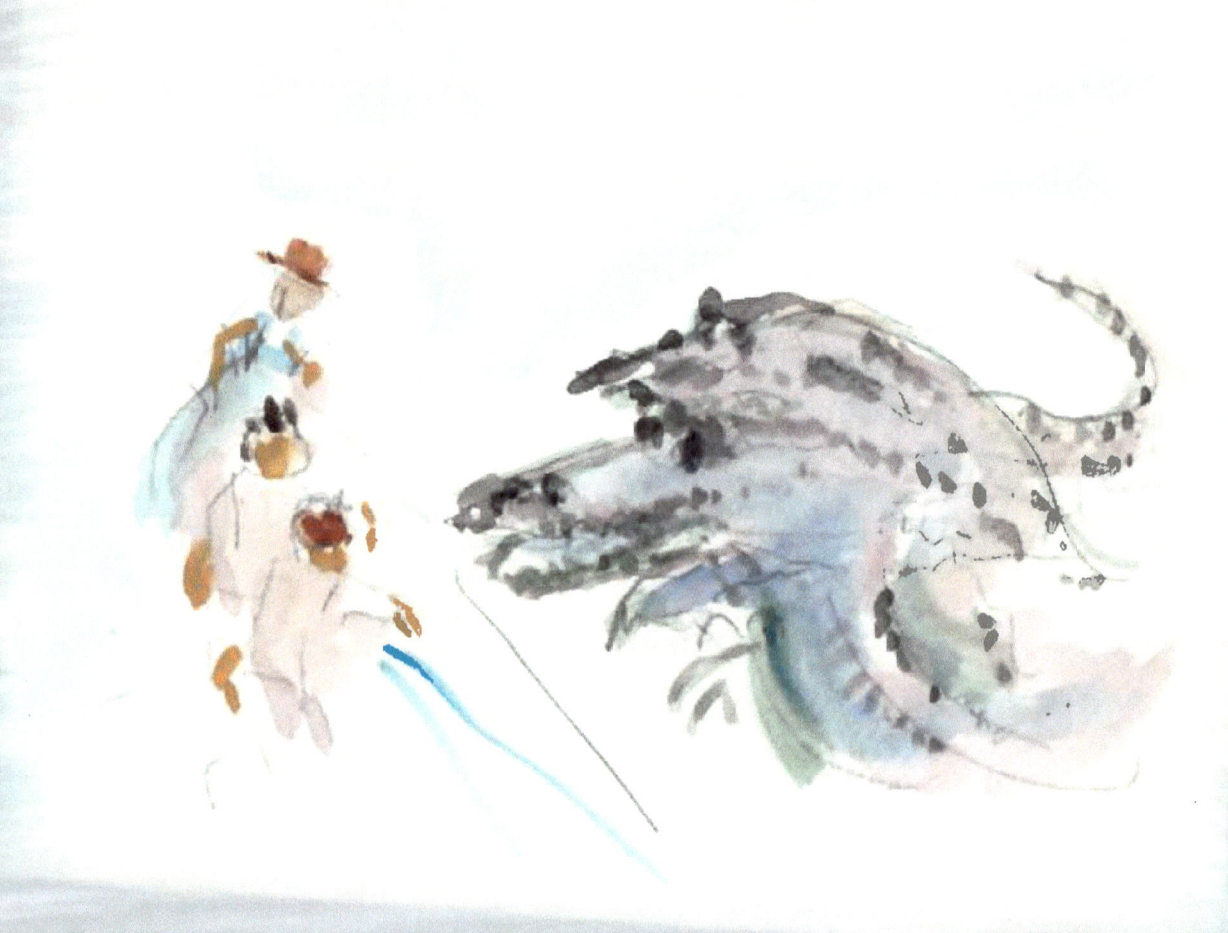

Mr. Joe Mr. Joe
then we checked out a croc
who was hiding out of sight.

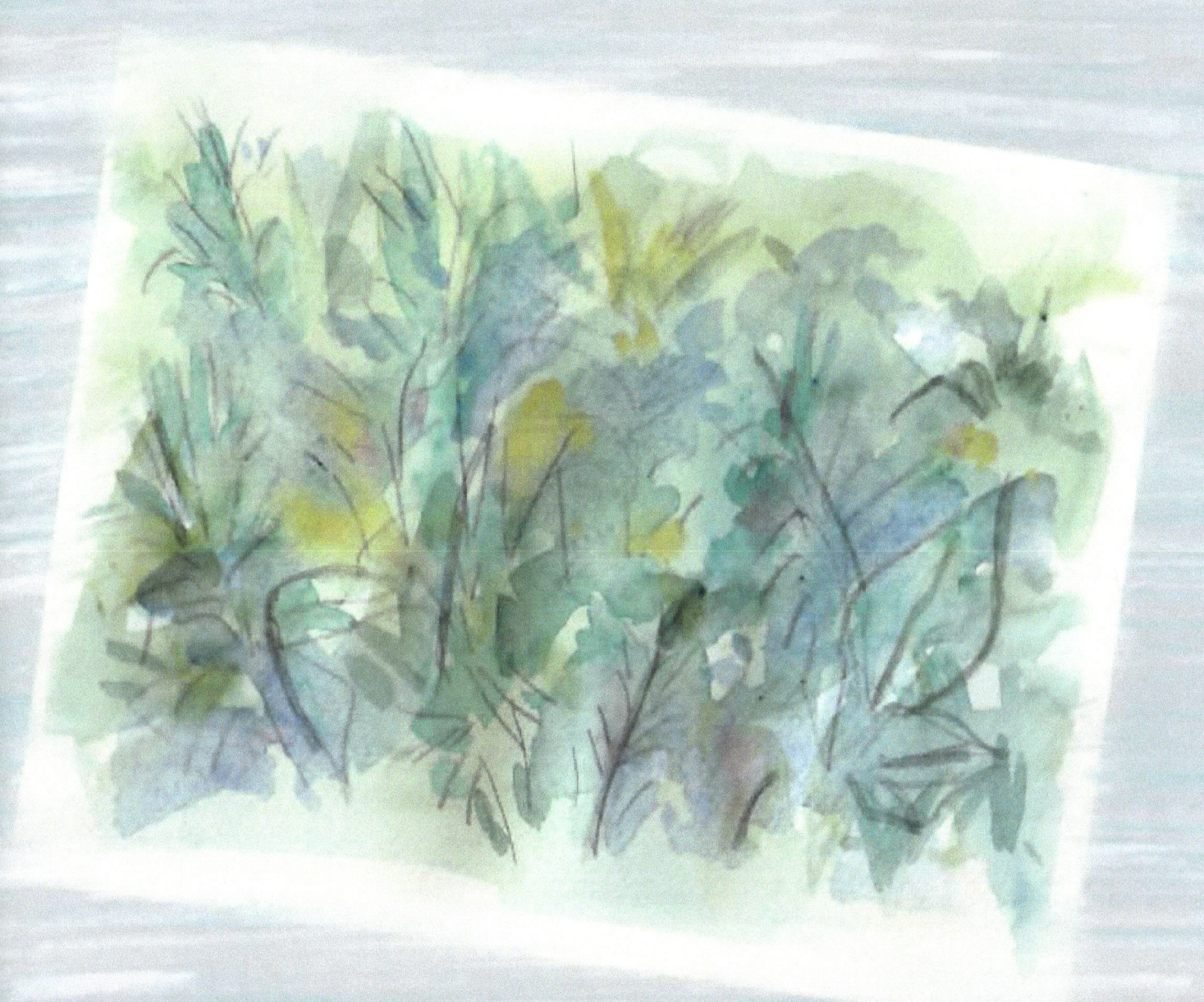

I guess it's better that it
was hiding because they
have a nasty bite!

Mr. Joe Mr. Joe
come with me for a
short jog.

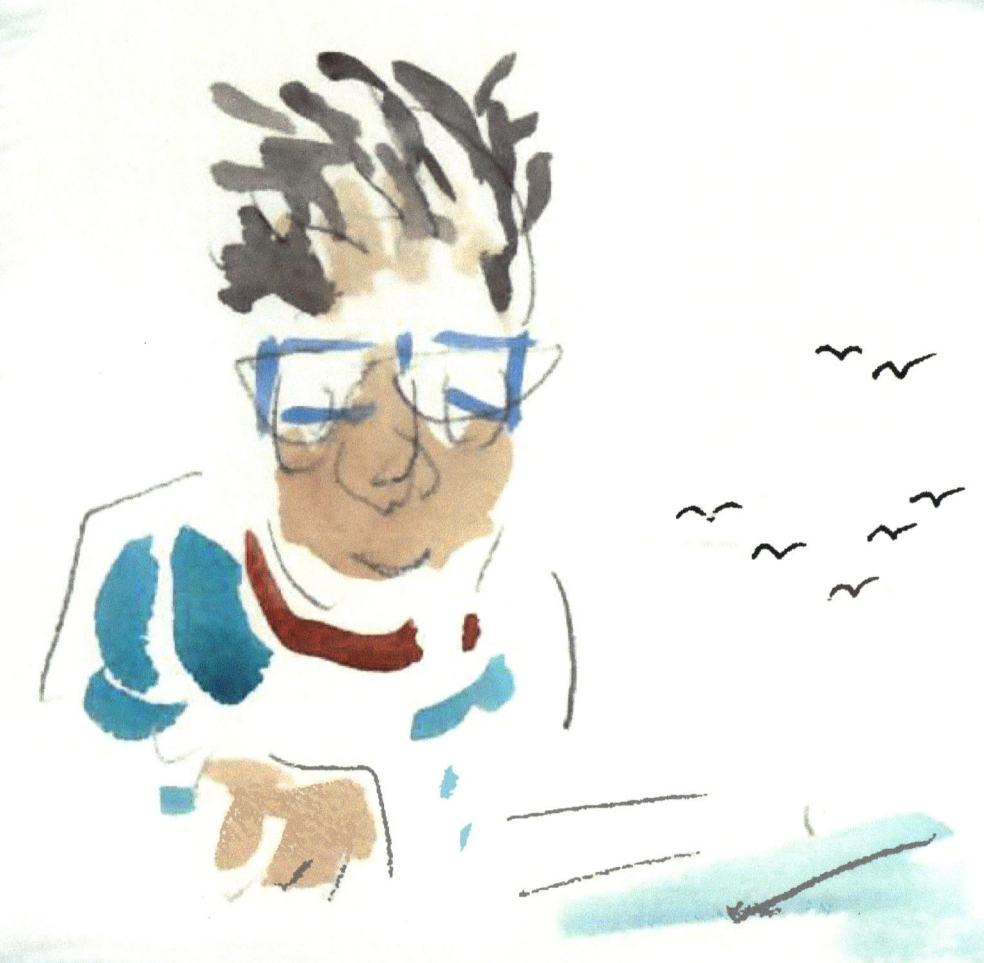

WAIT! Stop right there! Do you see the poison dart frog?

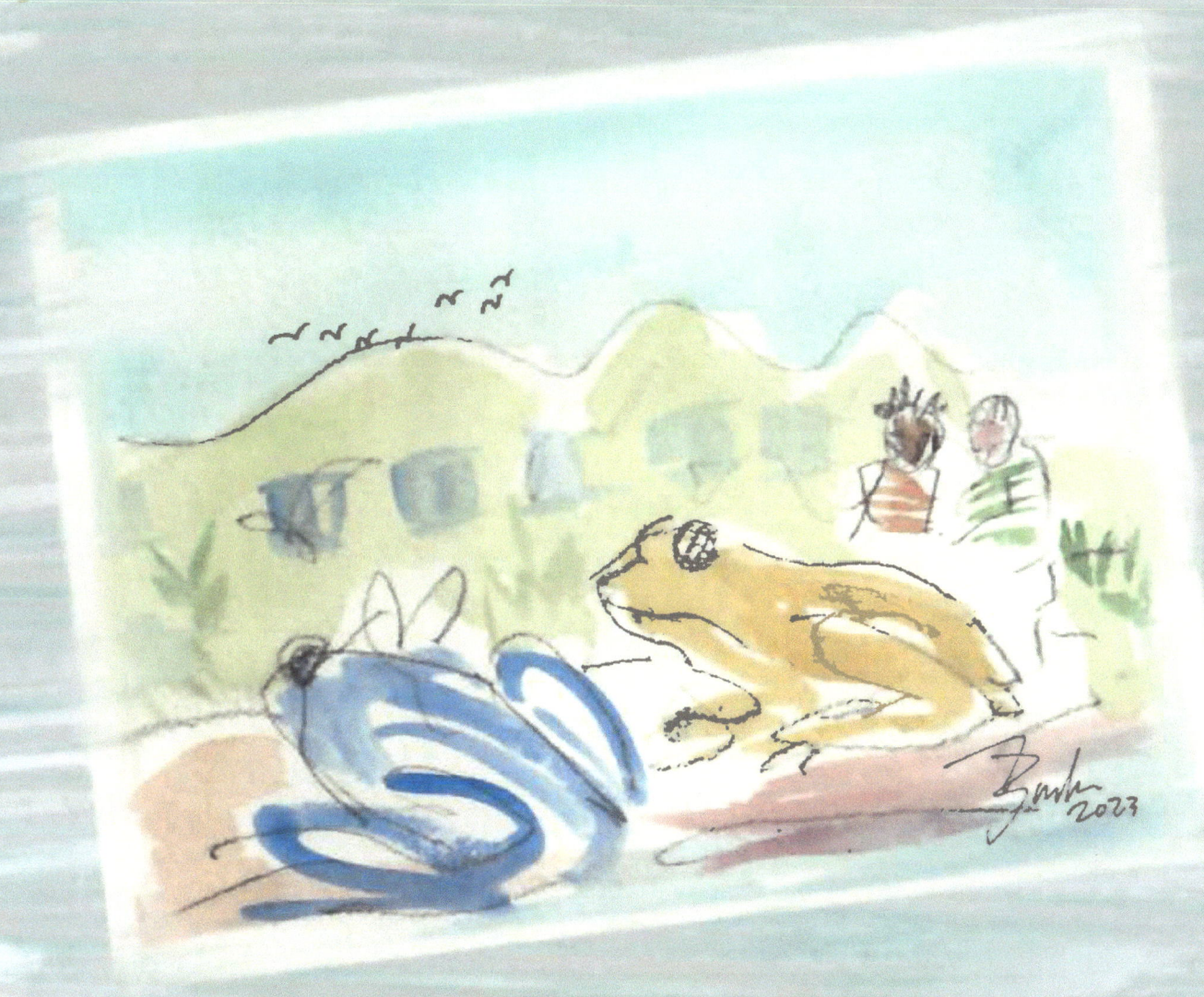

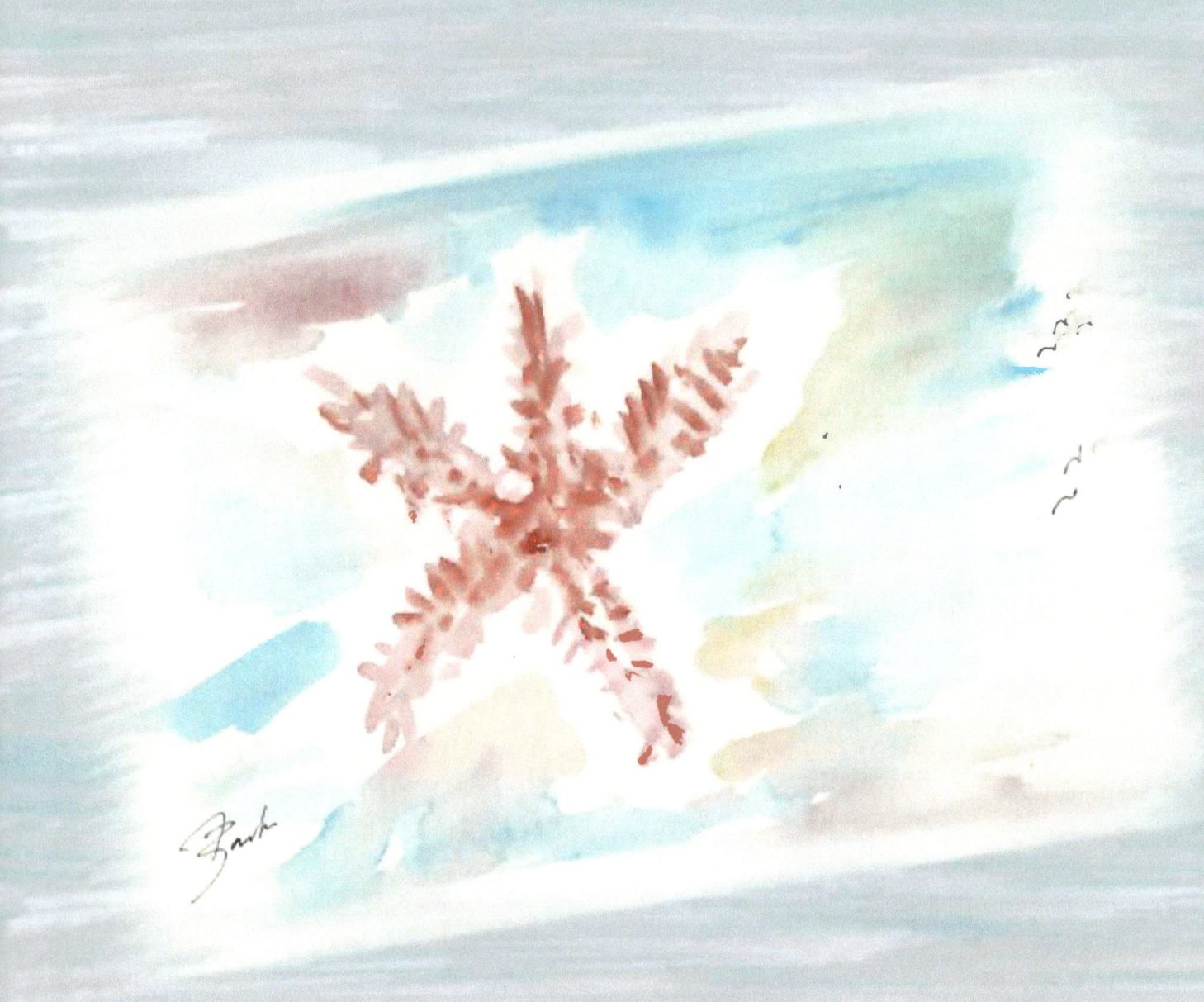

Mr. Joe Mr. Joe
check this out - you can
even touch a sea star!

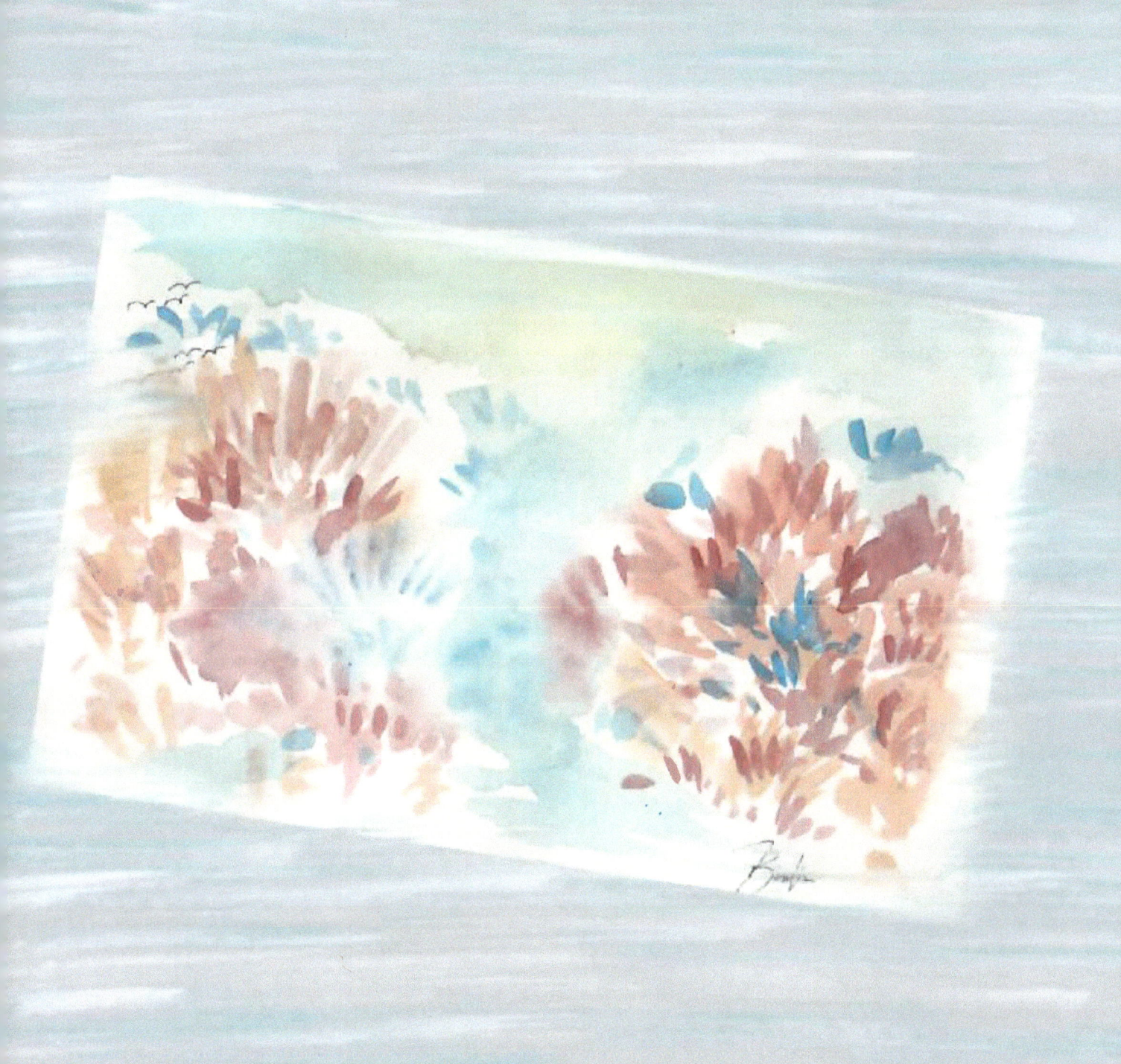

Oh STOP! Just touch it..
ewww it does feel a bit
bizarre.

Mr. Joe Mr. Joe
you won't believe what's in
the next exhibit.

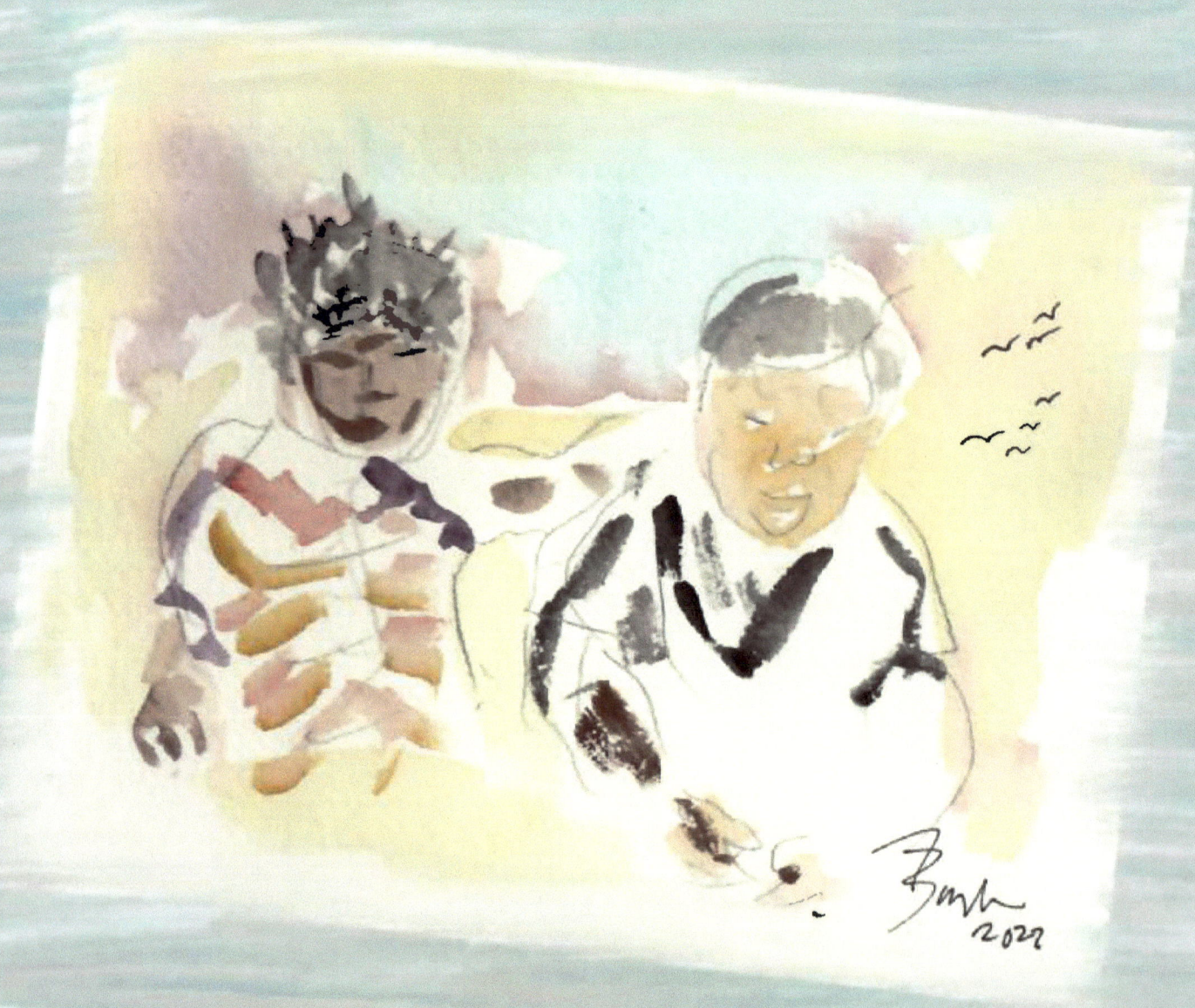

It's two fantastic hippos,
which touching them,
the aquarium does
prohibit.

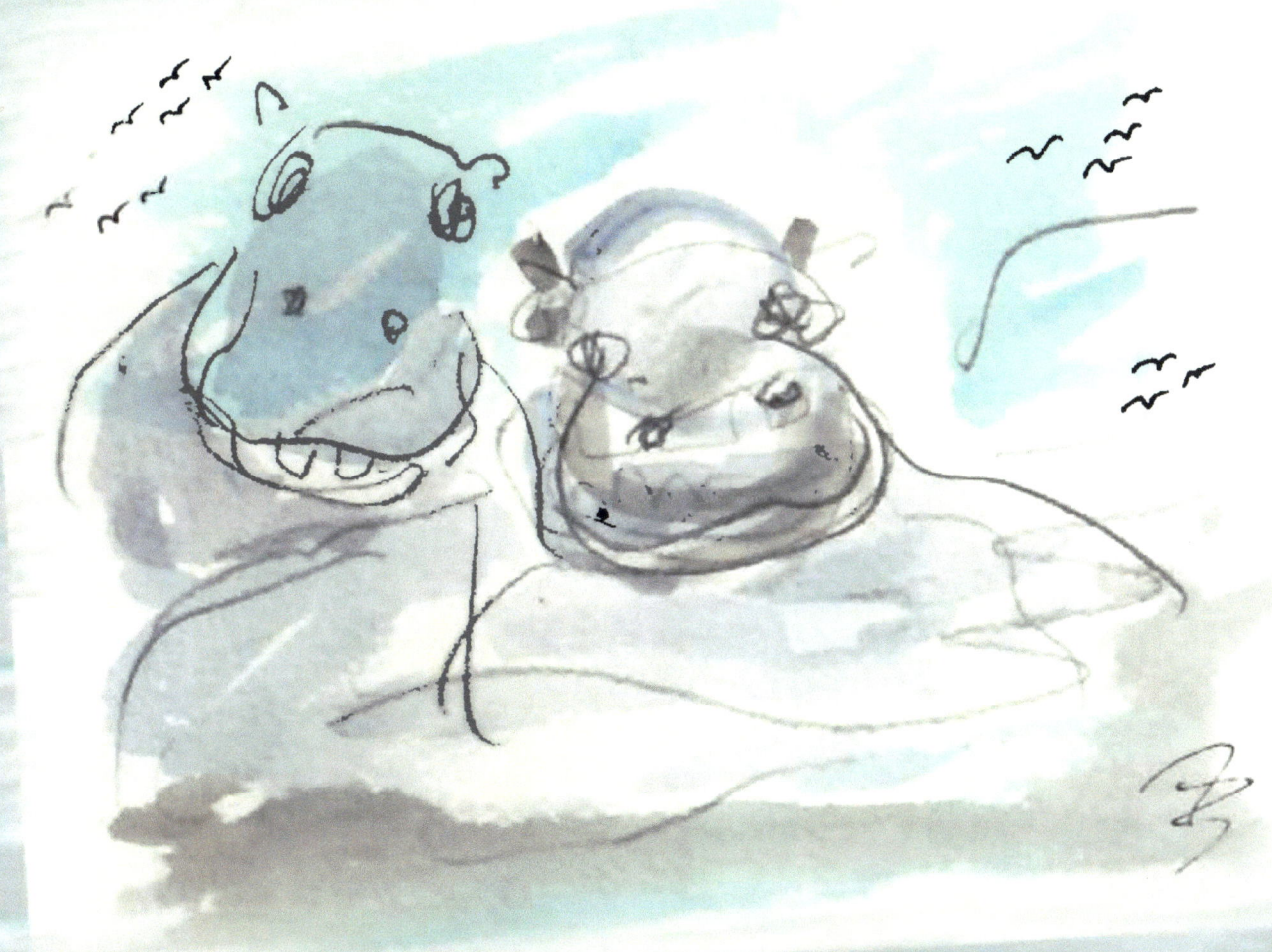

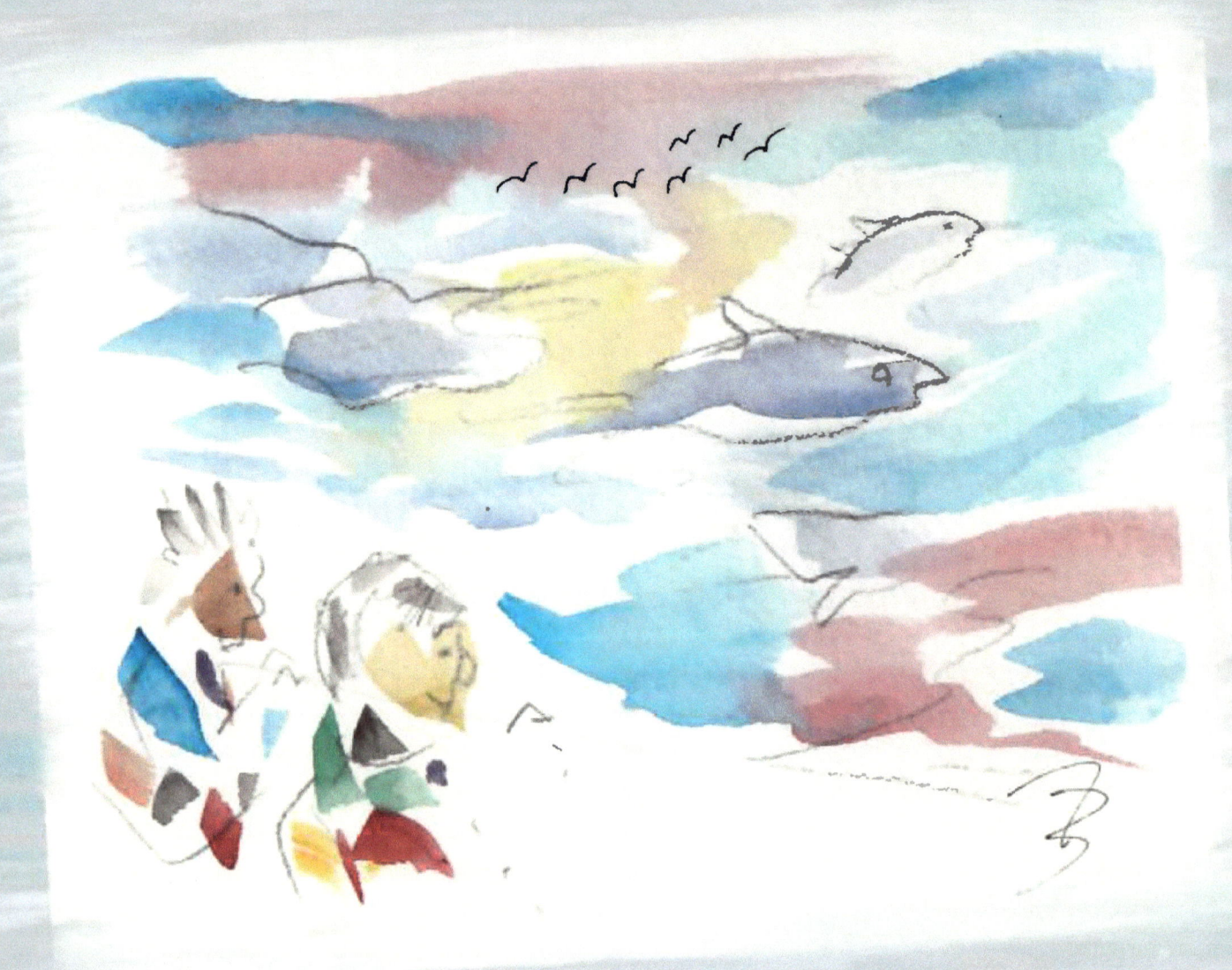

Mr. Joe Mr. Joe
the next area with a
megladon jaw is my
favorite to see.

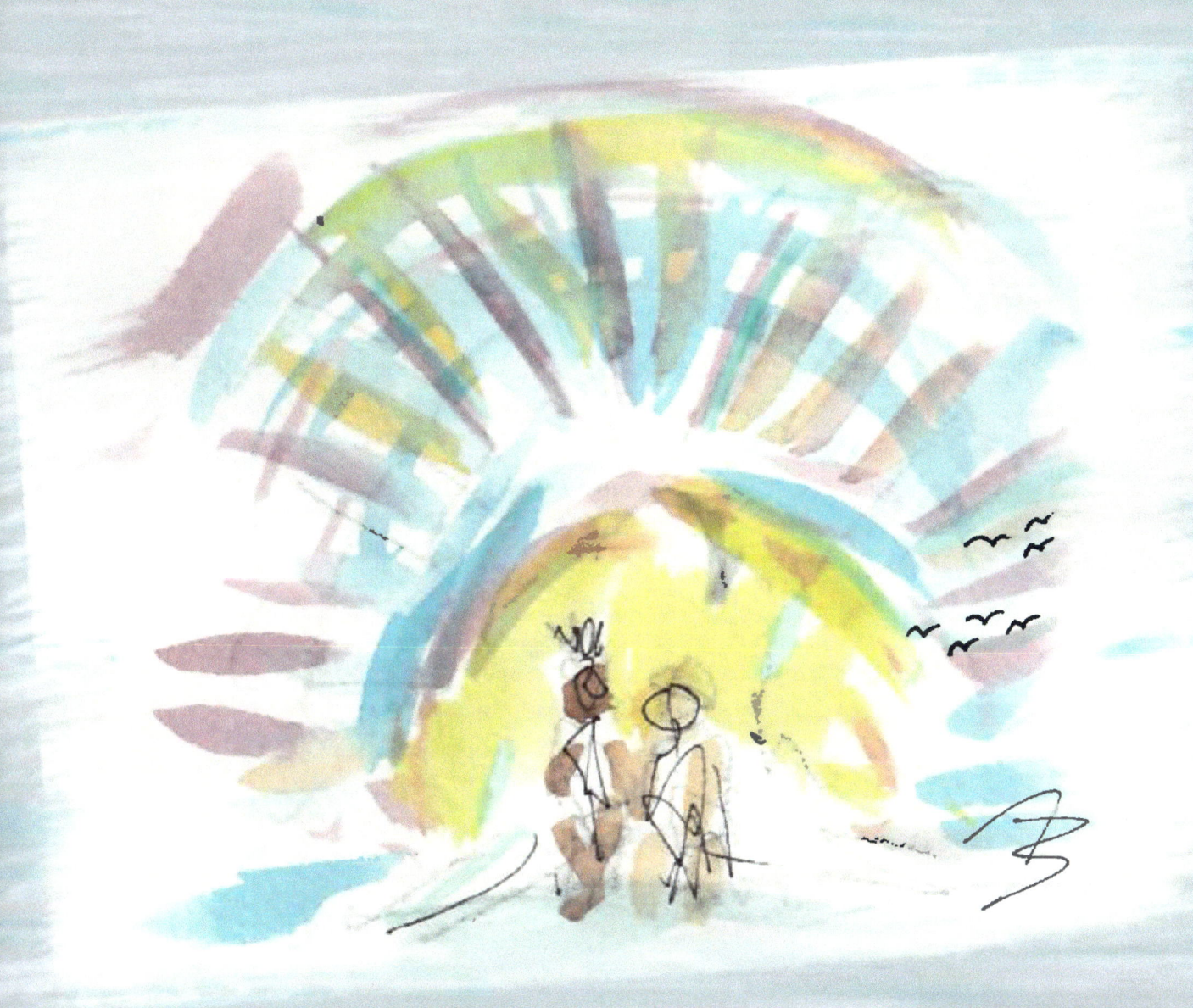

You will also love walking through the shark tunnel - I guarantee!

Mr. Joe Mr. Joe at the end of this exhibit is a shark bridge made of rope.

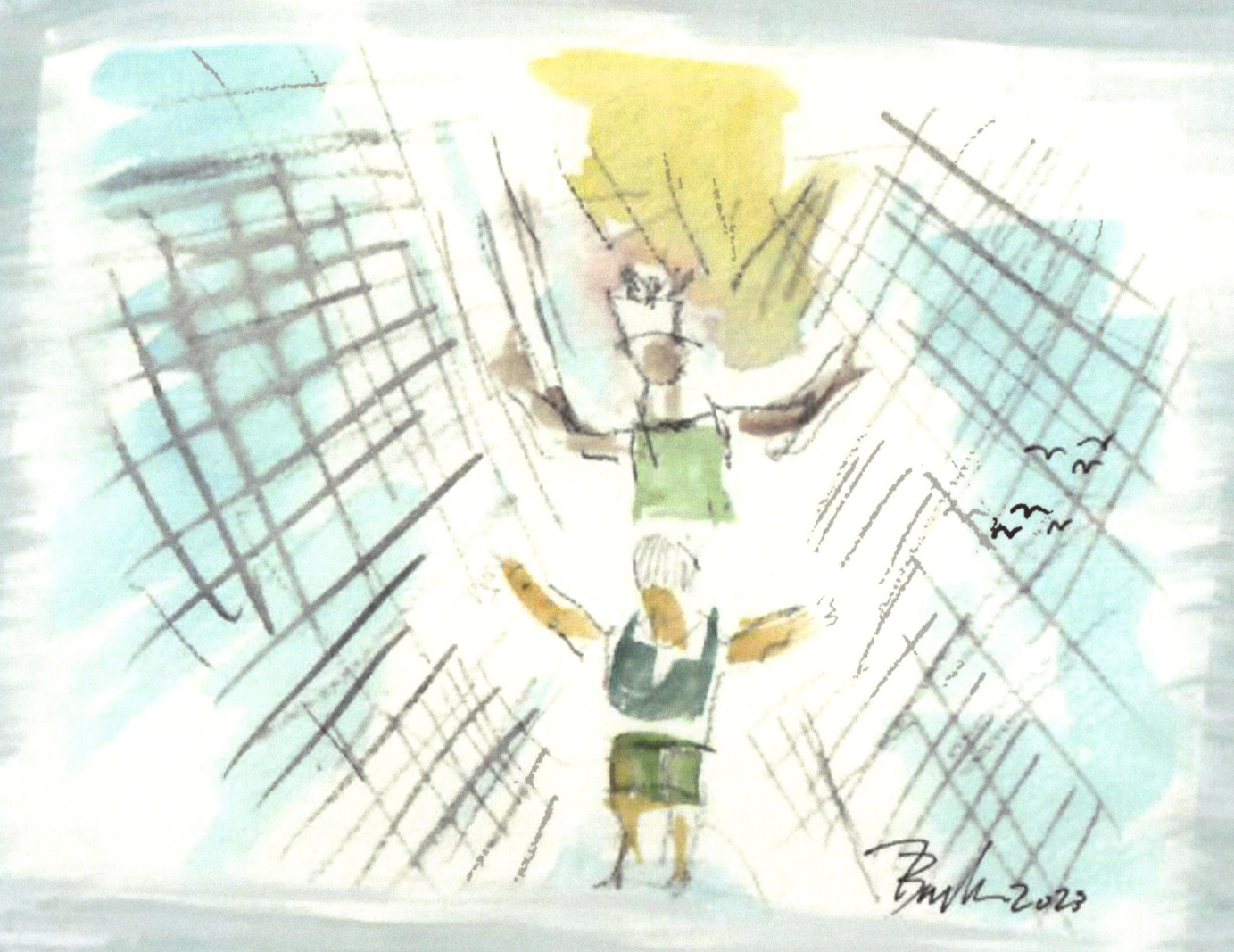

ALRIGHT! This time I'll be brave and say something other than NOPE.

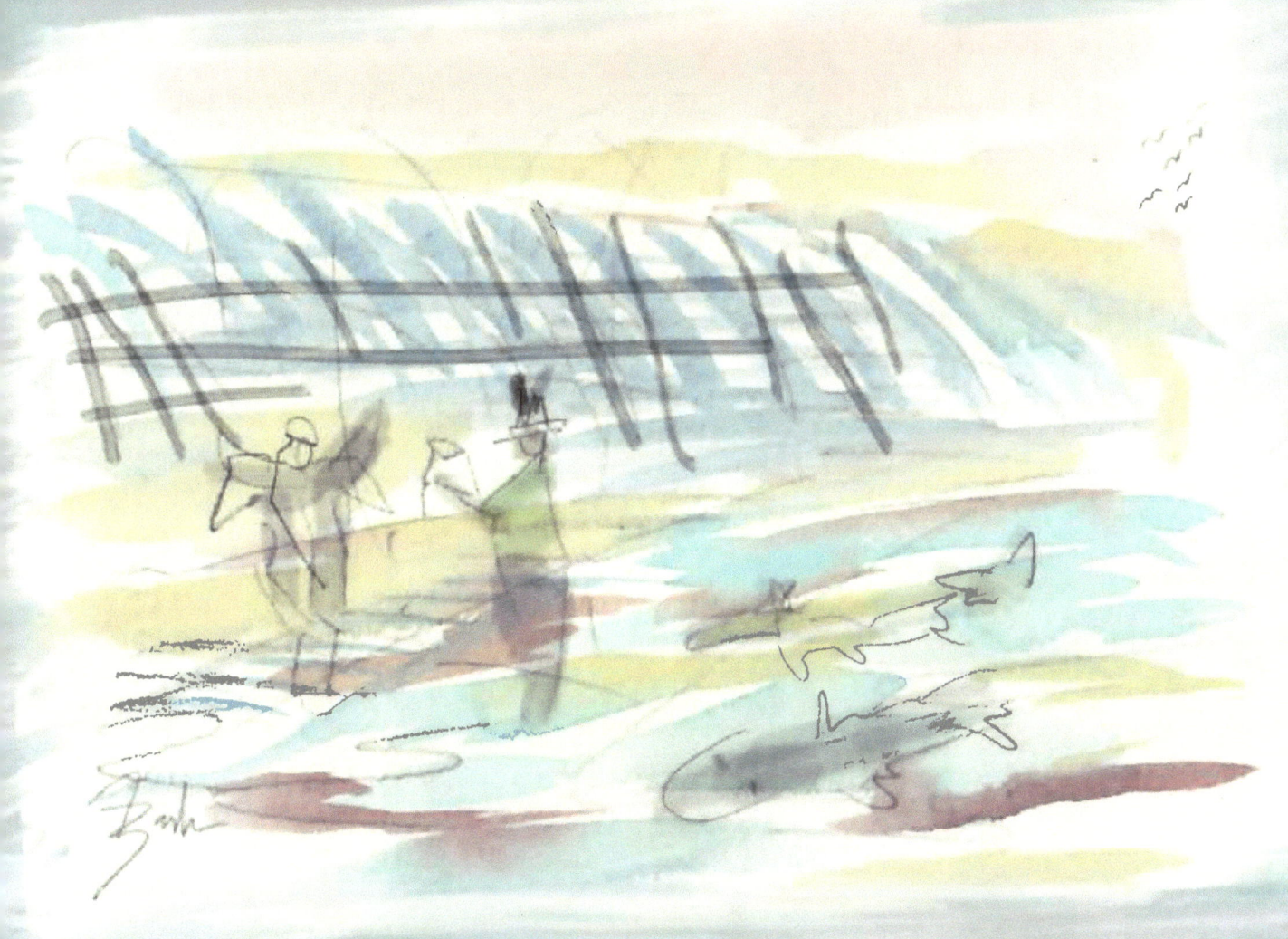

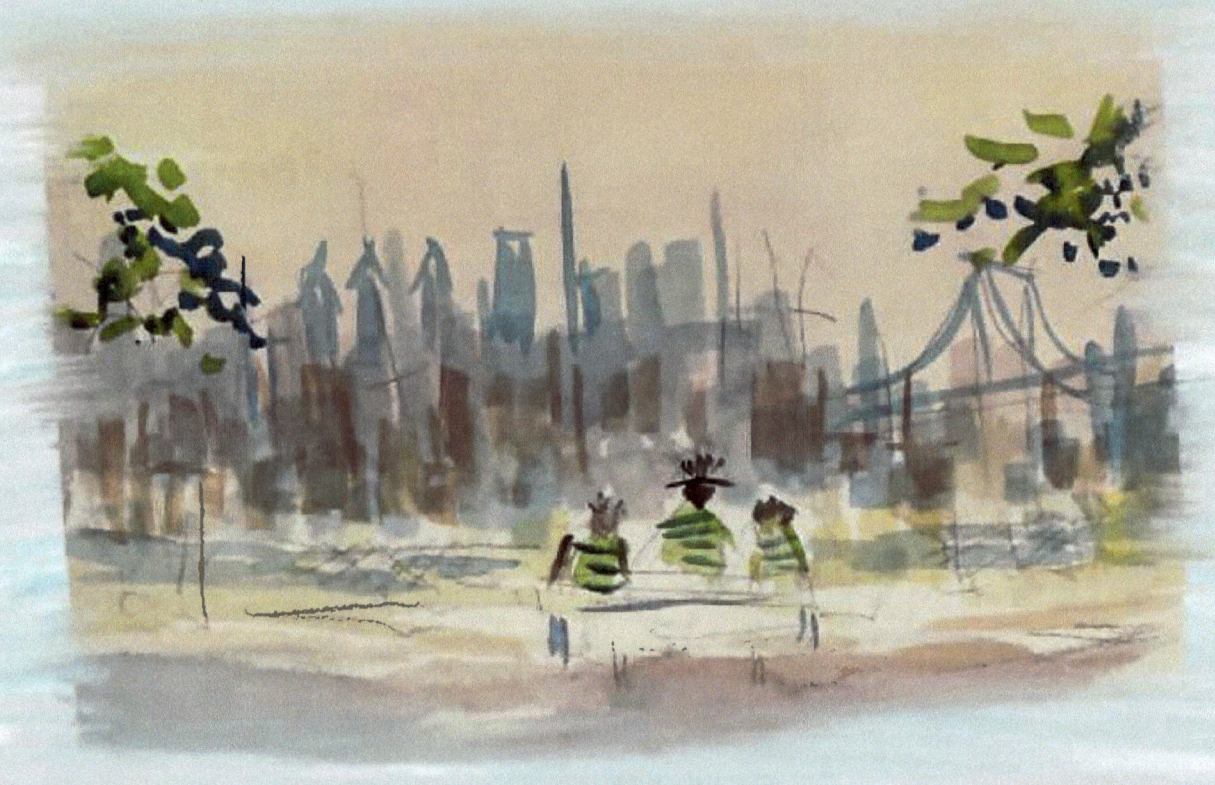

Mr. Joe Mr. Joe can you believe we explored every inch of the aquarium today?
I know it was a lot of walking, let's sit down on the bench this way.

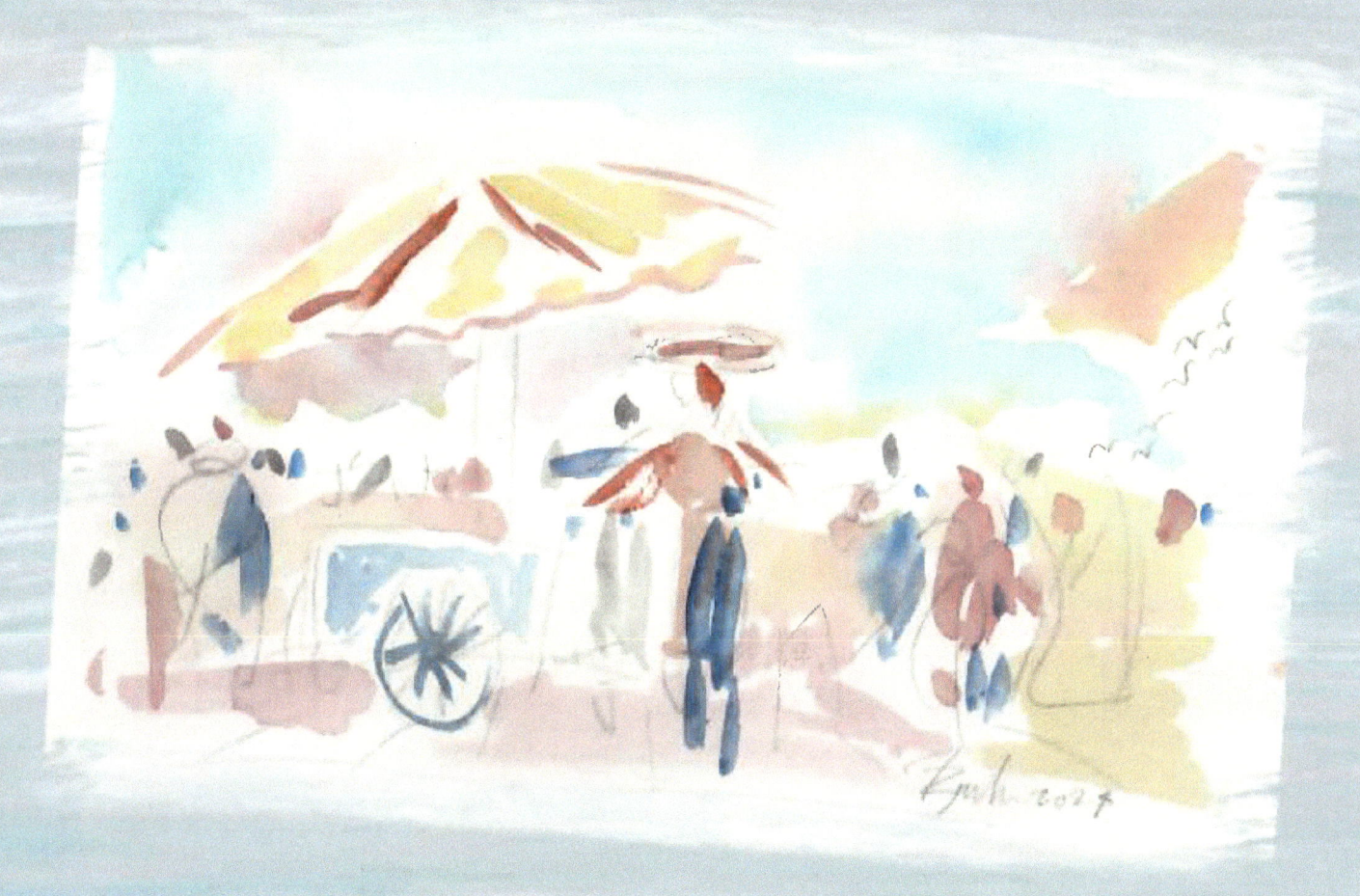

Mommy & brother will go
get lunch for us to eat.
Let's find a bench, look at
the waterfront and take a
seat!

Mr. Joe Mr. Joe lets get out of here it's starting to get chilly.

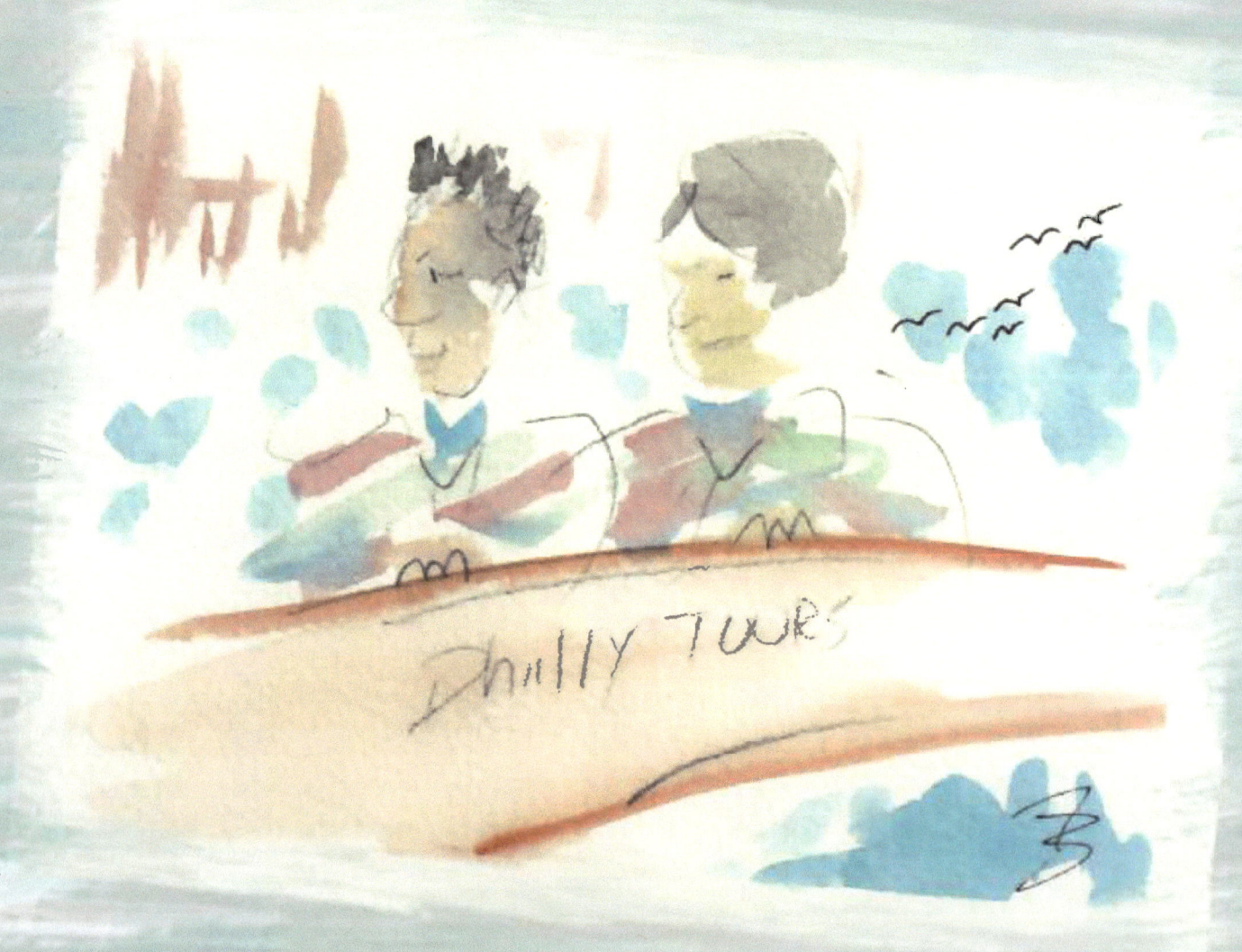

But before we take you home let's plan our next adventure. Can we go to Philly?????

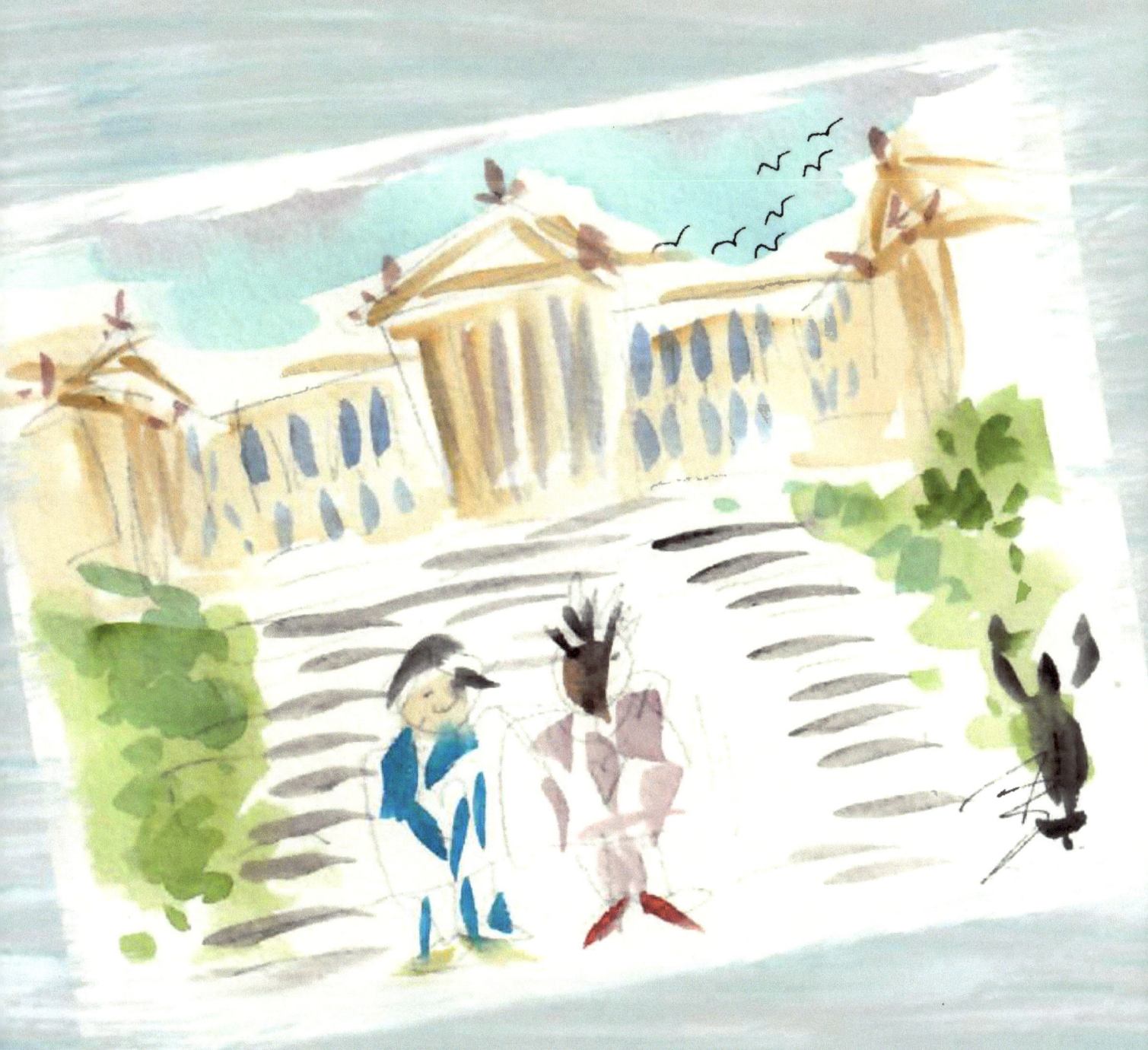